IS-245.A: Introduction to the Defense Priorities and Allocations System (DPAS)

By

Fema

10/31/2013

IS-245.a - DPAS Orientation Defense Priorities and Allocations System (DPAS)

Course Overview

The goal of this course is to promote basic understanding of the Defense Priorities and Allocations System (DPAS). A more advanced course provides detailed information on DPAS implementation. Upon completion of this course, you will be able to describe:

- How DPAS supports timely procurement of materials and services.

- How program officials use DPAS.

- Federal Emergency Management Agency (FEMA) and contractor responsibilities under DPAS.

- Procedures for placing priority-rated contracts and orders ("rated orders").

- Limitations on use of rated orders.

- Procedures for resolving DPAS issues.

What You'll Learn

In this course, you'll learn:

- DPAS supports the timely delivery of critical materials and services to meet program requirements through the use of priority-rated contracts and orders.

- DPAS has some limitations and may not be used to procure certain types of materials and services.

- Delivery problems for DPAS rated orders can be resolved through Special Priorities Assistance.

An Overview of DPAS Authorities

The statutory authority for DPAS is Section 101(a) of the Defense Production Act of 1950 (50 U.S. Code (U.S.C.) App. Sec. 2061, et seq.) (DPA), which authorizes the President to require priority performance of contracts or orders deemed necessary or appropriate to promote the national defense over any other contracts and orders. To ensure such priority, the President can require acceptance and performance of these contracts and orders by any person found capable of their performance.

Section 702(14) of the DPA defines the term "national defense" to mean programs for military and energy production or construction, military or critical infrastructure assistance to any foreign nation, homeland security, stockpiling, space, and any directly related activity. The term also includes emergency preparedness activities conducted pursuant to title VI of the Robert T. Stafford Disaster Relief and Emergency Assistance Act, As Amended (Stafford Act) and critical infrastructure protection and restoration.

The President delegated this DPA priorities authority under Executive Order (E.O.) 12919 to six Federal agencies:

- Department of Agriculture (USDA) for food resources;

- Department of Energy (DOE) for energy resources;

- Department of Health and Human Services (HHS) for health resources;

- Department of Transportation (DOT) for civil transportation;

- Department of Defense (DOD) for water resources (further delegated to the U.S. Army Corps of Engineers (USACE); and

- Department of Commerce (DOC) for all other materials, services, and facilities, including construction materials. These DOC resources are termed "industrial resources."

E.O. 12919 also established three agencies to make program determinations for priorities and allocations support:

- DOD for military-related programs;

- DOE for energy-related programs; and

- Department of Homeland Security (DHS) with respect to programs pertaining to "essential civilian needs supporting national defense, including civil defense and continuity of government." This includes programs to implement the Stafford Act authority as defined in title VI of that act, and for critical infrastructure protection and restoration (CIPR).

DOC is, at this time, the only one of the six agencies to have promulgated a regulation—the DPAS—to implement its delegated priorities authority. DOC has delegated to the Secretary of DHS under DPAS Delegation #4, the authority to use the DPAS to support DHS operational programs determined by DHS as eligible for this support. You will learn more about this Approved Program list later in this presentation. The Secretary of DHS has in turn delegated the authority to implement and administer the DPAS in DHS to the FEMA Administrator under DHS Delegation 9001. The FEMA Administrator has delegated this authority to other FEMA officials.

For further information regarding these authorities, please contact the Office of Policy and Program Analysis (OPPA) at

(202) 646-3350 or go to https://www.fema.gov/office-policy-program-analysis/defense-production-act-program.

Course Structure

This course includes the following major topics:

- FEMA's DPAS Authority

- DPAS Program Eligibility

- Use of DPAS Authority

- Limitations on DPAS Use

- Special Priorities Assistance

Target Audience

All FEMA personnel responsible for management and oversight of FEMA emergency management programs, including:

- FEMA program officials responsible for directing the use of DPAS priority ratings, and

- DPAS Officers appointed to advise and assist FEMA program officials in DPAS administration.

In addition, anyone interested in learning more about DPAS, such as Contracting Officers/Specialists, may complete this course.

FEMA Program Officials

Under "Delegation of Authority: Defense Priorities and Allocations System" from the FEMA Administrator, the authority to use DPAS priority ratings on contract and orders is further delegated to certain FEMA program officials.

These FEMA program officials include:

- Deputy Administrator, FEMA

- Deputy Administrator of National Preparedness and Protection

- Associate Administrator, Mission support

- U.S. Fire Administrator

- Regional Administrators

- Federal Insurance and Mitigation Administrator

- Associate Administrator, Operations

- Federal Coordinating Officers

- Director, Office of Policy and Program Analysis

The Director of OPPA is responsible for providing guidance, procedures, and coordination for the exercise of this delegated authority.

The authority delegated to the listed FEMA program officials may be re-delegated in writing to appropriate subordinate program officials.

Any questions about the exercise of this delegated authority should be directed to the Lead DPAS Officer, OPPA. See the contact information at the end of this course.

DPAS Officer Roles and Responsibilities

The role of DPAS Officers includes:

- Providing information and training on the use of DPAS,

- Attempting to resolve requests for Special Priorities Assistance (SPA), and

- Forwarding unresolved SPA requests to FEMA's Lead DPAS Officer in the Office of Policy and Program Analysis (OPPA).

FEMA's DPAS Authority

Key points to remember about FEMA's DPAS authority include:

- FEMA is delegated DPAS authority by the Department of Commerce to use priority ratings on contracts and orders to ensure timely delivery of "industrial resource" items (including performance of services) to meet FEMA's DPAS-eligible program requirements.

- The Director of FEMA's Office of Policy and Program Analysis (OPPA), under delegation from the FEMA Administrator, implements and administers this delegated DPAS authority as set forth in the FEMA DPAS Directive and Manual.

- A FEMA program official with DPAS authority must direct the use of DPAS priority ratings for FEMA program procurement activities.

- DPAS authority can be used without a Presidential emergency or major disaster declaration.

Definition of Industrial Resources

"Industrial resources" is defined in the FEMA DPAS Manual as:

"All materials (including construction materials), services, and facilities, except the following: (1) food resources, food resource facilities, and the domestic distribution of farm equipment and commercial fertilizer; (2) all forms of energy;

(3) health resources; (4) all forms of civil transportation; and (5) water resources."

[FEMA DPAS Manual FD 211-1-1, Chapter 1-5(VI)]

Because FEMA's DPAS authority can only be used to support the acquisition of Industrial Resources, FEMA officials wishing to use priority ratings on contracts and orders for food, energy, water, health care, or civil transportation should contact OPPA if there is a need to obtain any of these excluded resources.

We will discuss this limitation and others in the Limitations on DPAS Use section of this course.

What Is DPAS?

DPAS helps ensure the timely performance of contracts and orders placed in support of FEMA programs. The term "FEMA program" applies to a wide variety of activities supporting the FEMA mission of preparedness, response, and recovery.

Examples of FEMA programs include:

- **Preparedness** for a hurricane season, such as the procurement of critical items (e.g., generators, tarps) or equipment purchases, maintenance, and upgrades (e.g., communications, response support vehicles).

- **Response and recovery activities** by Federal Coordinating Officers (FCOs) or other FEMA program officials with DPAS authority.

DPAS Preparedness Example #1

DPAS plays an important role in emergency preparedness. Let's look at a hypothetical example of a preparedness program that might be authorized for DPAS support.

Case Example: FEMA received funding to upgrade its emergency radio system. Given the mandated deadline, the program official wants to minimize the risk of delays and requests DPAS authority for the program. The Deputy Administrator for National Preparedness and Protection directs the use of priority ratings, allowing the program to place rated orders to help ensure timely delivery and installation of the radio equipment.

DPAS Preparedness Example #2

A second example of DPAS support for preparedness programs is the upgrade of communication and power equipment.

Case Example: The National Response Coordination Center (NRCC) has been advised that its computer equipment and emergency power systems are aging and subject to failure, which could shut down the entire facility. The NRCC Director requests the Associate Administrator of Operations to direct the use of priority ratings on rated orders to help ensure the timely delivery of needed equipment upgrades prior to hurricane season.

DPAS Response Example

DPAS also supports critical pre-incident response activities. Let's look at a hypothetical example.

Case Example: Just after landfall of Hurricane Ike, the Director of the Logistics Management Directorate (LMD) identified a list of critical items to procure, including Mobile Disaster Recovery Center (MDRC) units, Logistics Support Vehicles, generators, and tarps.   The FEMA Assistant Administrator for Operations (a FEMA program official with rating authority) authorized the LMD Director to direct the placement of priority-rated contracts and orders to acquire the materials, as they were essential to support disaster response and recovery operations, in high demand, and only available in limited quantities.

The authorization allowed the LMD Director to use the DPAS for:

- The procurement of critical items to meet timely delivery dates, and

- Anticipated procurement needs for critical items considered essential to support the Agency's response and recovery mission.

How Does DPAS Help?

Under DPAS, when a rated order is placed with a contractor, the contractor must:

- **Accept the rated order** if the ordered material or service is normally supplied.

- **Provide preferential delivery or performance** against the rated order to the extent necessary to meet the delivery or performance date(s) specified in the order.

- **Place rated orders with subcontractors** and suppliers to obtain the materials and services needed to support the rated order.

Subcontractors and suppliers, in turn, must place rated orders with their vendors and lower tier suppliers, and so on throughout the entire chain of industrial supply, thus ensuring timely delivery of end items.

DPAS supports the timely delivery of critical items and services to meet program requirements.

What FEMA Programs Are Eligible?

Most FEMA activities are eligible for DPAS support, including:

- Federal emergency preparedness, response, and recovery.

- Similar activities to support State, local, and tribal governments.

- Critical infrastructure protection and restoration.

A FEMA program official with DPAS authority directs the use of DPAS priority ratings to support a program.

OPPA is available to provide guidance on program eligibility for DPAS authority.

Using DPAS Authority

The next section of this course presents the process for using the authority to place DPAS rated orders.

FEMA program officials should consider using DPAS authority when there is an emergency preparedness, response, or recovery requirement, and a limitation on DPAS use is not applicable to procurement of the required item(s) (limitations are discussed later in this course).

DPAS will help ensure timely delivery of critical materials if, for example*:

- The program has a hard or mandated deadline, or

- There are known or potential procurement or performance problems.

***Note:** These situations are not required in order to use DPAS authority.

Placing Rated Orders

Now that you understand the process for using DPAS authority, the next section will explain how DPAS is implemented.

If the program is eligible, a FEMA program official with DPAS authority:

- Directs a FEMA Contracting Officer/Specialist to place rated orders for the materials or services, and

- Provides information on the required quantities and delivery dates.

Then, the Contracting Officer/Specialist includes specific, required language in the solicitation and contract.
The program official will submit a quarterly Report of DPAS Use to OPPA.

The procedures for initiating a rated order can be summarized by two key decision points:

1. First, the program must be determined eligible and a program official with DPAS authority must direct the use of DPAS priority ratings. (Most FEMA programs are eligible.)

2. If the program is eligible, the program official must then determine if each acquisition activity is eligible for a DPAS priority rating. If so, he/she directs the

Contracting Officer/Specialist to include a DPAS clause in the contract or order.

Solicitation Clause for Rated Orders

For RFQ and IDIQ solicitations that will be issued as rated orders, the Contracting Officer/Specialist is required to include a clause, described below in the FAR.

TITLE 48 - FEDERAL ACQUISITION REGULATIONS SYSTEM
CHAPTER 1 - FEDERAL ACQUISITION REGULATION
SUBCHAPTER H - CLAUSES AND FORMS
PART 52 - SOLICITATION PROVISIONS AND CONTRACT CLAUSES

<u>52.211 - 14 - Notice of Priority Rating for National Defense Use</u>.

As prescribed in 11.604(a), insert the following provision:

Notice of Priority Rating for National Defense Use (SEP 1990)

Any contract awarded as a result of this solicitation will be a [ ] DX rated order; [ ] DO rated order certified for national defense use under the Defense Priorities and Allocations System (DPAS) (15 CFR part 700), and the Contractor will be required to follow all of the requirements of this regulation.

[Contracting Officer check appropriate box.]

(End of provision)

[51 FR 19717, May 30, 1986, as amended at 55 FR 38518, Sept. 18, 1990.

Redesignated and amended at 60 FR 48251, 48256, Sept. 18, 1995]

Required Elements in a Rated Order

For rated contracts and procurement orders, the Contracting Officer/Specialist must include four required elements, described below in the DPAS Regulation (15 CFR 700).

<u>§ 700.12 Elements of a rated order</u>.

Each rated order must include:

(a) The appropriate priority rating (e.g. DO-A1, DX-A4, DO-H1);

(b) A required delivery date or dates. The words "immediately" or "as soon as possible" do not constitute a delivery date. A "requirements contract", "basic ordering agreement", "prime vendor contract", or similar procurement document bearing a priority rating may contain no specific delivery date or dates and may provide for the furnishing of items from time-to-time or within a stated period against specific purchase orders, such as "calls", "requisitions", and "delivery orders". These purchase orders must specify a required delivery date or dates and are to be considered as rated as of the date of their receipt by the supplier and not as of the date of the original procurement document;

(c) The written signature on a manually placed order, or the digital signature or name on an electronically placed order, of an individual authorized to sign rated orders for the person placing the order. The signature or use of the name certifies that the rated order is authorized under this part and that the requirements of this part are being followed; and

(d) A statement that reads in substance: This is a rated order certified for national defense use, and you are required to follow all the provisions of the Defense Priorities and Allocations System regulation (15 CFR part 700).

[49 FR 30414, July 30, 1984. Redesignated at 54 FR 601, Jan. 9, 1989, as amended at 63 FR

31922, June 11, 1998]

The rated order statement is further described below, in the Federal Acquisition Regulation (FAR).

TITLE 48 - FEDERAL ACQUISITION REGULATIONS SYSTEM

CHAPTER 1 - FEDERAL ACQUISITION REGULATION

SUBCHAPTER H - CLAUSES AND FORMS

PART 52 - SOLICITATION PROVISIONS AND CONTRACT CLAUSES

<u>52.211-15 Defense Priority and Allocation Requirements</u>.

As prescribed in 11.604(b), insert the following clause:

Defense Priority and Allocation Requirement (Apr 2008)

This is a rated order certified for national defense, emergency preparedness, and energy program use, and the Contractor shall follow all the requirements of the Defense Priorities and Allocations System regulation (15 CFR 700).

(End of clause)

Priority Ratings

One of the required elements in a rated contract or order is the priority rating. A priority rating in a FEMA rated order consists of:

- **A "DO" priority level,** which is the level used for all DHS/FEMA DPAS rating authorizations, and

- **A program identification symbol (PIS),** which is one of eight PIS identifiers numbered "N1" through "N8".

Most FEMA programs will use a DPAS priority rating of "DO-N1," which is for Federal emergency preparedness, response, and recovery.

DPAS Priority Levels

The DPAS provides for two levels of rated order priority: "DX" and "DO". DX rated orders take precedence over DO rated orders and unrated orders (commercial orders without a DPAS priority rating), as necessary to meet the delivery or performance requirements of the DX orders. DO rated orders only take precedence as necessary over unrated (commercial) orders as necessary to meet delivery or performance requirements of the DO rated orders. All DX rated orders have equal priority with each other and all DO rated orders have equal priority with each other.

Under DPAS Delegation #4 from DOC to DHS, DHS is permitted only to use the DO level of priority. The DX level of priority is reserved for use by DOD to support our Nation's most critical weapons system programs and may not be used by DHS.

The symbols "DX" and "DO" are not acronyms for any terms. They simply indicate the level of priority.

For further information about the DPAS levels of priority, please contact OPPA at (202) 646-3350 or go to https://www.fema.gov/office-policy-program-analysis/defense-production-act-program.

Current DHS-Approved Program Identification Symbols Under DPAS

- N1: Federal emergency preparedness, mitigation, response, and recovery

- N2: State, local, and tribal government emergency preparedness, mitigation, response, and recovery

- N3: Intelligence and warning systems

- N4: Border and transportation security

- N5: Domestic counter-terrorism, including law enforcement

- N6: Chemical, biological, radiological, and nuclear countermeasures

- N7: Critical infrastructure protection and restoration

- N8: Miscellaneous

Again, most FEMA programs will use a DPAS priority rating of "DO-N1," which is for Federal emergency preparedness, response, and recovery.

Limitations on DPAS Use

DPAS is only used to support contracts and orders to procure "industrial resources." DPAS may **NOT** be used:

- For contracts and orders for food, energy, water, health care, or civil transportation service. (Contact OPPA if there is a need to obtain any of these excluded resources.)

- To procure items that meet **all three** of the following criteria ("common use" items):

    o Are commonly available in commercial markets for general consumption,

    o Do not require major modification when purchased, **and**

    o Are readily available in sufficient quantities to meet program requirements.

- To procure items for administrative use.

Therefore, DPAS priority rated orders do not apply when using purchase cards to buy "cash and carry" items at retail stores. By definition, such transactions are not considered orders and the items are readily available.

Excluded Resources

The FEMA DPAS Manual (FD 211-1-1) at Chapter 3-3(III) states:

"DPAS priority ratings may not be used to procure: (1) food resources, food resource facilities, and the domestic distribution of farm equipment and commercial fertilizer; (2) all forms of energy; (3) health resources; (4) all forms of civil transportation; and (5) water resources. Program officials wishing to place rated orders for any of these resources should contact the Lead DPAS Officer, Office of Policy and Program Analysis (OPPA) for assistance."

For example, bottled water is not an "industrial resource" subject to the DPAS. It is a "water resource" under the jurisdiction of the Defense/U.S. Army Corps of Engineers (DOD/USACE). Therefore, a FEMA program official who needs to obtain rating authority to procure bottled water should contact OPPA to request this authority from the DOD/USACE.

Similarly, meals-ready-to-eat (MREs) are not an "industrial resource" subject to the DPAS. They are "food resources" under the jurisdiction of the Department of Agriculture (USDA) and a FEMA official who needs to obtain priority rating authority to procure MREs should contact OPPA to request this authority from the USDA.

"Common Use" Items

DPAS Delegation #4 to DHS prohibits a rated order from being used to procure any item(s) if all three of the following limitations apply (note the "and" at the end of the second bullet):

The item(s):

- Are commonly available in commercial markets for general consumption,

- Do not require major modification when purchased, and

- Are readily available in sufficient quantities to meet program requirements.

Accordingly, if an item is commonly available in the commercial market for general consumption, and the item does not require major modification when purchased, but the item is not readily available in sufficient quantities to meet a requirement of a DPAS eligible program (e.g., response or recovery from a disaster), then a rated order may be placed to procure the item.

For example, tarps are a commonly available item in commercial markets for general consumption. However, in an emergency situation, if tarps are not readily available in sufficient quantities to meet emergency requirements, a rated order may be used to support tarp acquisition.

"Administrative Use" Items

Rated orders may not be used to procure any administrative use items, such as items needed for financial or personnel management. This limitation would normally include use of rated orders to procure office furniture and equipment that is not directly needed in support of a DPAS eligible program requirement.

For further information about the use of rated orders for common use items and the restriction on their use for excluded resources and administrative items, please contact OPPA.

Special Priorities Assistance (SPA)

Although DPAS is designed to be largely self-executing, it provides for special priorities assistance (SPA) to address procurement problems that can occur generally after placement or attempted placement of a rated order with a contractor.

SPA may be used for such purposes as:

- Expediting deliveries.

- Resolving delivery conflicts between or among rated orders.

- Placing rated orders with contractors and suppliers.

- Identifying potential contractors and suppliers.

- Verifying information provided by contractors and suppliers.

Contact the program or component DPAS Officer for SPA coordination. If a DPAS Officer is not available, contact the Lead DPAS Officer in OPPA.

Requesting SPA

SPA can help address a number of problems with a rated order or contract.

It is important to understand that anyone involved with the rated order may request SPA, including the program official, the Contracting Officer/Specialist, the DPAS Officer, or the contractor, subcontractors, or lower-tier suppliers.

Regardless of who is requesting SPA, the process is the same. The person making the request will:

1. Document the request using Form BIS-999 (with OPPA assistance, if needed).

2. Submit it, along with any supporting information and documentation, to a DPAS Officer.

The DPAS Officer will then immediately contact OPPA to resolve the issue.

FEMA DPAS Manual FD 211-1-1

CHAPTER 4 – RESOLUTION OF ISSUES RESULTING FROM USE OF PRIORITY RATINGS

4-1 <u>Special Priorities Assistance (SPA)</u>

I.   General

FEMA components and contractors may need assistance in obtaining timely delivery of needed items or authority to use a priority rating on orders for items not normally eligible for priority rating. Sections 700.50 through 700.55 of the DPAS regulation provide for Special Priorities Assistance.

II.   Requesting SPA

A.   Any contractor, program official, Contracting Officer, or DPAS Officer may request SPA for a variety of reasons. (See 15 CFR 700.52 for examples and 15 CFR 700.54 for instances where assistance may not be provided.)

B.   Requests for SPA should be made as soon as the affected person has made a reasonable effort to resolve the problem, but failed.

C.   In general, a SPA request should be submitted to a DPAS Officer within the FEMA component responsible for the impacted program. If a DPAS Officer has not been designated for the component, a request may be submitted to the Lead DPAS Officer, OPPA.

D. DPAS Officers may prepare a request for SPA or may assist a contractor in preparing a request.

E. Requests for SPA shall be submitted using Form BIS-999, which is available electronically at www.bis.doc.gov or in hard copy.

1. The contractor or DPAS Officer must complete blocks 1 through 7 on Form BIS-999 and have an authorized official sign the certificate in block 8.

2. All information provided as part of a request for SPA should be unclassified. If classified information must be included, such material must be transmitted and handled according to appropriate security procedures.

III. Assistance Rendered by DPAS Officers

A. The cognizant DPAS Officer should attempt to resolve a SPA request. If unable to do so, the DPAS Officer should forward the request to the Lead DPAS Officer, OPPA. All requests for SPA must be fully documented to demonstrate a need for the requested assistance.

B. Prior to forwarding SPA requests to the Lead DPAS Officer, DPAS Officers shall:

1. Ensure that reasonable efforts to resolve the problem(s) have been made by the involved contractor and program official(s).

2. Confirm that the contractor is unable to obtain the required item(s) in a timely fashion to meet program requirements.

3. Document in Form BIS-999 or in an attachment thereto, all actions taken at every level to process and resolve the SPA request.

4. Confirm that the required documentation and information is complete, accurate, and valid. SPA requests must:

   a. Provide evidence that there is an urgent need for the item(s) addressed in the request to meet program requirements.

   b. State the consequences of failure to obtain timely delivery of the item(s).

   c. Demonstrate that the required item(s) cannot be replaced by other item(s) that could serve the same purpose effectively.

   d. Demonstrate that the contractor cannot sustain the necessary production without timely delivery of the needed item(s).

   e. Document all problems for which SPA is being requested.

5. Confirm, when applicable, that provisions for mandatory or optional rejection of a rated order as set forth in section 700.13 (b) and (c) of the DPAS regulation do not

apply and that assistance is not prohibited. (See section 700.54 of the DPAS regulation.)

Note: Section 700.54 of the DPAS Regulation describes instances where assistance will not be provided, including situations when a person is attempting to:

a. Secure a price advantage;

b. Obtain delivery prior to the time required to fill a rated order;

c. Gain competitive advantage;

d. Disrupt an industry apportionment program in a manner designed to provide a person with an unwarranted share of scarce items; or

e. Overcome a supplier's regularly established terms of sale or conditions of doing business.

SPA Example

SPA can help resolve conflicts and delivery delays after a rated order has been placed.

Case Example: For instance, the Joint Field Office (JFO) in Baton Rouge has placed a rated order with a contractor/producer of emergency generators and switching equipment because of the upcoming hurricane season. The contractor reports that the supplier of switching equipment cabinets is unable to meet the contractor's delivery requirement, and thus, the contractor will not be able to deliver the generator and switching equipment to meet the FEMA requirement.

The JFO Procurement Unit contacts the regional DPAS Officer for assistance.

DPAS Officers

The DPAS Officer:

- Plays a key role in resolving any SPA or other concerns with rated orders.

- Is a FEMA employee designated by the head of a FEMA component to address, as a collateral duty, DPAS issues and support program officials and Contracting Officers/Specialists.

The role of DPAS Officers includes:

- Providing information and training on the use of DPAS,

- Attempting to resolve requests for SPA, and

- Forwarding unresolved SPA requests to FEMA's Lead DPAS Officer in OPPA.

OPPA works to resolve the referred SPA requests. If OPPA is unable to resolve the SPA request, it may be referred to the Department of Commerce for resolution.

For More Information

For more information about DPAS implementation or administration, including eligibility of FEMA programs for DPAS support or SPA issues:

- Contact FEMA's Lead DPAS Officer.

  - Through OPPA: (202) 646-3350

- o   By Email: FEMA-DPAS@dhs.gov

- Visit the Defense Production Act Program Division Web site at: https://www.fema.gov/office-policy-program-analysis/defense-priorities-and-allocations-system-dpas.

- Complete the second Independent Study course in this series, "Implementing DPAS in FEMA Operations" available through the Emergency Management Institute.